P9-EDX-614

j567.9
Fisher, Enid.
The great dinosaur record
book

ALLEN COUNTY PUBLIC LIBRARY
FORT WAYNE, INDIANA 46802

You may return this book to any agency or branch
of the Allen County Public Library

4/99

DEMCO

THE GREAT DINOSAUR RECORD BOOK

For a free color catalog describing Gareth Stevens' list of high-quality books and multimedia programs, call 1-800-542-2595 (USA) or 1-800-461-9120 (Canada). Gareth Stevens Publishing's Fax: (414) 225-0377. See our catalog, too, on the World Wide Web: gsinc.com

Library of Congress Cataloging-in-Publication Data

Fisher, Enid.
   The great dinosaur record book/by Enid Fisher; illustrated by Richard Grant.
      p.   cm. — (World of dinosaurs)
   Includes bibliographical references and index.
   Summary: Identifies the biggest dinosaur, the smallest, the fastest, the most intelligent, and other record-holders among these prehistoric animals.
   ISBN 0-8368-2176-9 (lib. bdg.)
   1. Dinosaurs—Miscellanea—Juvenile literature. [1. Dinosaurs—Miscellanea.] I. Grant, Richard, 1959- ill. II. Title. III. Series: World of dinosaurs.
QE862.D5F53   1998
567.9—dc21   98-23073

This North American edition first published in 1998 by
Gareth Stevens Publishing
1555 North RiverCenter Drive, Suite 201
Milwaukee, Wisconsin 53212 USA

This U.S. edition © 1998 by Gareth Stevens, Inc.
Created with original © 1998 by Quartz Editorial Services, 112 Station Road, Edgware HA8 7AQ U.K.
Additional end matter © 1998 by Gareth Stevens, Inc.

Consultant: Dr. Paul Barrett, Paleontologist, Specialist in Biology and Evolution of Dinosaurs, University of Cambridge, England.

All rights reserved. No part of this book may be reproduced, stored in a retrieval system, or transmitted in any form or by any means, electronic, mechanical, photocopying, or otherwise without the prior written permission of the copyright holder.

Printed in the United States of America

1 2 3 4 5 6 7 8 9 02 01 00 99 98

Allen County Public Library
900 Webster Street
PO Box 2270
Fort Wayne, IN 46801-2276

THE GREAT DINOSAUR RECORD BOOK

by Enid Fisher
Illustrated by Richard Grant

Gareth Stevens Publishing
MILWAUKEE

CONTENTS

INTRODUCTION

Welcome to the Great Dinosaur Record Book! In this fourth fact-packed title in a new, fully illustrated series, we introduce some of the most spectacular of these remarkable prehistoric creatures. And, we predict, you will be in for lots of surprises!

Did you know, for instance, that there is fossil evidence to show that one kind of dinosaur had an amazingly long neck that extended 49 feet (15 meters)? Or that the heaviest of the dinosaurs may have weighed 100 tons? Some meat-eating dinosaurs had enormous fangs. And the very fastest of the dinosaurs could probably run about 40 miles (65 kilometers) per hour.

What you may find amazing, too, is that not all the dinosaurs were huge. In fact, some were just the size of today's chickens.

Many dinosaurs, although large, had tiny brains and may have been low in intelligence. Others, however, had larger brains, and scientists believe they might have been very intelligent. Some, we can tell from fossilized remains, were extremely noisy, bellowing to each other with mating calls or warnings of imminent danger. Others relied on powerful tails, bony head helmets, or razor-sharp claws to defend themselves or to attack prey.

Which three dinosaurs, then, might have been at the top of each of these categories? No one will ever know for certain, but, based on fossil records, we have ventured to choose what we consider the most remarkable. We now invite you to meet and become acquainted with these outstanding, amazing, prehistoric record-breakers.

A MONSTER TO MARVEL AT

We can only imagine the size of what many experts believe was the largest dinosaur. Nothing as huge exists on Earth today. Even the mighty elephant would have to grow to at least twice its size to look this prehistoric giant in the eye!

The ground shook, and tall trees shivered. Bloodcurdling roars tore the calm of the warm Cretaceous day, sending frightened creatures scurrying into dense thickets. Suddenly, a pair of enormous jaws lined with razor-sharp teeth appeared out of the undergrowth, gaping and snapping viciously. **Giganotosaurus** was very hungry and on the prowl.

What a terrifying beast it was! At 40 feet (12 meters) in length and three times as tall as today's average adult male human, **Giganotosaurus** was one of the largest and fiercest dinosaurs ever to roam our planet.

New record-breaker

When pieced together by experts, the fossilized remains of **Giganotosaurus** — found in Argentina, in South America, in 1995 — form a carnivore that must have been taller than **Tyrannosaurus rex**, formerly thought to have been the largest dinosaur of all!

Giganotosaurus's head sat on a short, sinewy neck supported by slender shoulders. It had a powerful body and a massive tail, at least 15 feet (4.5 m) in length, which extended straight out behind it when **Giganotosaurus** ran at top speed.

Giganotosaurus chased and killed not only smaller carnivores but also herbivores of all sizes, bringing them down and biting large chunks of flesh from their fallen bodies. Fossilized remains of plant-eaters, such as **Titanosaurus** and armored **Saltosaurus** — both of which were discovered in the same area as **Giganotosaurus** — indicate that there was probably plenty of food available for a creature of such an incredible size.

TOP THREE FIERCEST

1st: Giganotosaurus
Cretaceous; found in
Argentina, South America;
40 feet (12 m) long

2nd: Tyrannosaurus rex
Cretaceous; found in
North America and eastern
Asia; 39 feet (12 m) long

3rd: Allosaurus
Jurassic; found in North
America, Australia, and
Africa; 36 feet (11 m) long

SMALL BUT NOT CUTE

Dinosaurs came in all shapes and sizes, but, surprisingly, some of the most vicious were the smallest! They may have looked harmless because of their size, but evidence shows they packed a nasty bite.

A lizard lay basking in the Late Jurassic sunshine. The cleverly camouflaged creature felt it was safe to snooze; with its coloring, it could hardly be seen against the forest floor. All at once, however, the morning's calm was broken by a rustling sound. Within seconds, eager hand claws gripped the lizard's body and stuffed it headfirst between wide, yawning jaws. **Compsognathus** (*opposite*) had caught its first meal of the Jurassic day!

Tiny thug

Ready for breakfast, this early predator was only 2 feet (60 centimeters) long — smaller than Triassic **Procompsognathus**. It had long back legs that could carry it at high speeds, while its shorter forelimbs were armed with claws.

Even flying creatures were not safe when **Compsognathus** was out for the kill. It had a long neck it could extend to catch flying insects, which could then be crushed within its jaws. Tiny **Coelurus**, from North America was only 6 feet (1.8 m) long, and scientists believe it had habits similar to **Compsognathus**.

Mini-cannibals

Compsognathus was fierce, but **Coelophysis**, an earlier predator from Late Triassic times (about 225 million years ago), may have been even more ferocious. In fact, **Coelophysis** may have been a cannibal! Paleontologists discovered the skeletons of several young **Coelophysis** in the stomach cavities of adult fossils that were dug up at Ghost Ranch, in New Mexico, in 1947.

Coelophysis was somewhat larger than **Compsognathus**, at 7 feet (2.1 m) in length. Like **Compsognathus**, it ran on two hind legs and grabbed prey with its sharp-clawed forelimbs. It

mainly ate small creatures, but the discovery of several of its skeletons together leads experts to believe they might have hunted in packs at times.

Better armed, however, was **Noasaurus**, another small dinosaur from Late Cretaceous times (some 150 million years later), whose skeletal remains have been unearthed in Argentina. This predator was 8 feet (2.4 m) long and had a curved sickle claw on each foot, which it could extend to slash at a victim.

Ornitholestes was a small Jurassic predator only 6.5 feet (2 m) long that had its eye on early birds. It was even given a name meaning "bird robber," because experts believed it could pluck flying creatures out of the sky using its strong jaws.

Many creatures — on the ground or in the air — must have fallen victim to these tiny terrors of prehistoric times!

TOP THREE TINIEST

1st: Compsognathus
Tiny, very swift, Jurassic carnivore; found in Germany and France; 2 feet (60 cm) long and just 6.5 pounds (3 kg)

2nd: Procompsognathus
Primitive Triassic carnivore; found in Germany; 4 feet (1.2 m) long

3rd: Coelurus
Slim Jurassic carnivore; found in Wyoming, in the U.S.; 6 feet (1.8 m) long

CHAMPION LONG-NECKS

Dinosaurs tended to have necks that suited their lifestyles. A meat-eater, for example, needed a short, flexible neck that it could lunge with when attacking its prey. Many of the larger sauropods that had to eat tons of plant food in order to survive evolved incredibly long necks.

Mamenchisaurus gazed over a wide Jurassic valley, in what is now the Szechwan province in China. For the moment, no other creature could be seen, although the bloodcurdling shriek of a hunting pterosaur high above sometimes broke the eerie silence of the landscape. **Mamenchisaurus**'s neck — all 49 feet (15 m) of it — was the longest of the Jurassic sauropods. Some experts think **Seismosaurus**, another sauropod, also had an extremely long neck, but they cannot adequately support the claim.

3 1833 03369 8314

Even mighty **Diplodocus** — one of the longest dinosaurs at 88 feet (27 m) from nose to tail — could manage only a mere 25 feet (7.5 m) of neck.

Mamenchisaurus held its head high in the air. An upward bend in the joints that linked the sturdy lower neck bones to the rest of this dinosaur's bulky body seems to indicate that this towering creature would have held its neck upright most of the time. Whenever **Mamenchisaurus** wanted a drink from a nearby pool or stream, it would have had to swing its neck down, just like the jib of one of today's mechanical cranes!

What a whopper!

You might think that such a long neck must have contained large bones but, in fact, they were not much bigger than the neck bones of other large dinosaurs — about 2 feet (60 cm) in length. There were, however, a lot more of them! **Mamenchisaurus** had as many as nineteen bones in its neck, whereas a meat-eater, such as **Tyrannosaurus rex,** which lived during Cretaceous times, would have had a lot less.

Tyrannosaurus rex, of course, did not need a long neck to feed. It could easily bend down to feed off the carcasses of prey. But a large plant-eater, such as

Mamenchisaurus, had to eat large quantities of vegetation to keep going. Its long neck enabled the herbivore to stretch up to heights where no other dinosaur could feed. Here, it could enjoy a meal in peace and quiet!

TOP THREE LONG-NECKS

1st: Mamenchisaurus
Jurassic sauropod; found in China; up to 88 feet (27 m) in length with a 49-foot (15-m)-long neck

2nd: Giraffatian
Jurassic sauropod; found in Tanzania, Africa; name means "gigantic giraffe;" possibly 33-foot (10-m)-long neck

3rd: Diplodocus
Jurassic sauropod; found in North America; up to 88 feet (27 m) in length with a 25-foot (7.5-m)-long neck

HEAVYWEIGHT CHAMPION

Many of the sauropod dinosaurs, which lived mainly in Jurassic times, were extremely heavy. Their weight when fully grown often exceeded that of several elephants. The largest of them all was Seismosaurus.

All the creatures in the Late Jurassic valley stopped what they were doing. Plant-eaters stopped browsing, and ferocious meat-eaters, poised for the kill, froze in midbite as the ground trembled beneath their feet.

As the steady rumbling continued, they were suddenly confronted by a creature so tall that it almost blocked the sun. **Seismosaurus** was passing through, and as its gargantuan feet crashed on the ground, the vibrations seemed to shake the very insides of Earth!

In 1985, scientists in New Mexico, in the United States, made a

1st: Seismosaurus
Late Jurassic sauropod; found in New Mexico, USA; over 100 feet (30 m) long and weighing over 100 tons; possibly the heaviest creature ever

2nd: Brachiosaurus
Jurassic sauropod; found in North America and Tanzania, Africa; up to 82 feet (25 m) long and weighing about 50 tons; distinctive high-placed nostrils

3rd: Apatosaurus
Jurassic sauropod; found in North America and Mexico; up to 70 feet (21 m) long and weighing more than 20 tons; formerly known as **Brontosaurus**

remarkable discovery — the remains of what is believed to be the heaviest dinosaur. From the few fossilized bones they found in the prehistoric riverbed, they estimated that **Seismosaurus** may have been over 100 feet (30 m) long. **Brachiosaurus** and other large sauropods now looked small in comparison. The paleontologists who discovered these massive bones have estimated its weight at over 100 tons, fourteen times as heavy as **Tyrannosaurus**, which tipped the scale at a mere 7 tons.

Earthshaker

Seismosaurus — its name means "earthshaker" — had the build of a typical sauropod, with a long neck that it carried almost horizontally except when eating. It also had a short, bulky body; square, pillarlike legs; huge, flat feet with a claw on the first toe; and a very long, tapering tail.

Smooth, shiny stones discovered by scientists in the stomach area of its skeleton show that **Seismosaurus** must have eaten tough vegetation, swallowing its food whole because it was unable to chew. It then used these smooth stones, called gastroliths, to grind up the plant material it needed to digest. Some paleontologists have gone so far as to claim that an adult Seismosaurus could munch its way through a ton of food each day in order to keep going!

Brachiosaurus was the previous heavyweight champion at 50 tons, but paleontologists believe that other weighty dinosaurs could have walked the Earth during Jurassic times. These massive, potential "challengers" have been named **Supersaurus** and **Ultrasaurus** by scientists. However, since only a handful of bones of each have been found, the theory is, as yet, only speculation. Is it possible that an even heavier — and more magnificent — creature is yet to be discovered?

FASTEST BY FAR

Most of the larger dinosaurs were heavily built, so they moved around slowly. Many of the smaller ones, however, were leaner and longer-limbed, looked similar to ostriches, and could run at speeds that match the swiftest animals alive today.

Whoosh! What was that? A lone baby **Ankylosaurus**, which had strayed from the side of its mother, heard a noise in the distance. Suddenly, it turned and saw a group of **Dromiceiomimus** racing toward it. These small, ostrichlike creatures were zooming in for the kill at 40 miles (65 km) per hour — about the average speed of a car today. They began to tear at their victim's flesh even before they had screeched to a halt.

The baby **Ankylosaurus** would soon be dead.

Other dinosaurs would also have found it easy to catch such a straggler. **Gallimimus**, for instance, could reach up to 35 miles

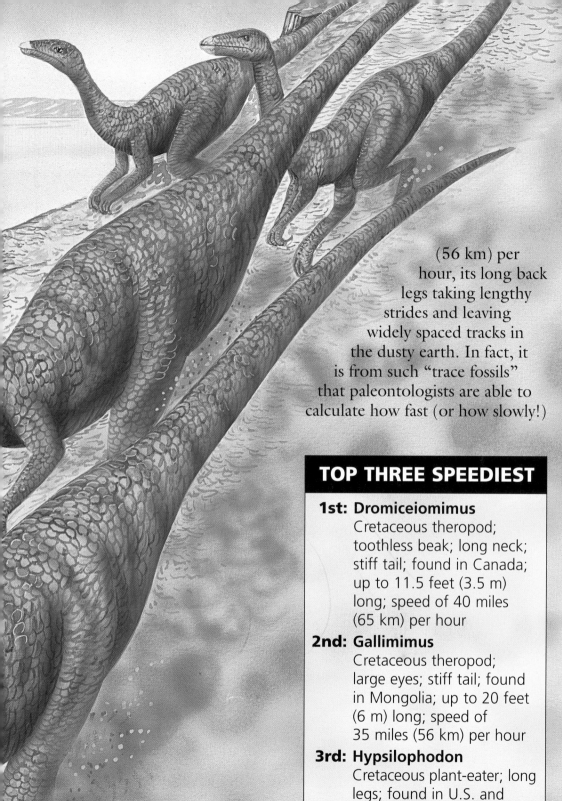

certain types of dinosaurs must have traveled around the prehistoric planet.

The heavier species, carrying weight of up to 50 tons, left tracks that were close together, indicating that they lumbered along, probably at no more than 5 miles (8 km) per hour.

Odds-on winner

Smaller, lighter dinosaurs, however, left tracks that were about 6.5-10 feet (2-3 m) apart, showing that they could run at high speeds. Experts even believe that **Dromiceiomimus** could have kept pace with a modern racehorse at full gallop — and that the fleet-footed dinosaur would have won such a race!

Most of the time, dinosaurs used their speed to chase and catch prey. Some, however, such as **Hypsilophodon**, were plant-eaters from Early Cretaceous times. They would probably have broken into a sprint to escape from predators. They could race through the landscape at an impressive 31 miles (50 km) per hour.

Next time you have an opportunity to see films of today's big cats, such as cheetahs and leopards, dashing across open plains after gazelles or wildebeest, try to picture them as dinosaurs. Then you will have some idea of what the baby **Ankylosaurus** had to face on that prehistoric day.

(56 km) per hour, its long back legs taking lengthy strides and leaving widely spaced tracks in the dusty earth. In fact, it is from such "trace fossils" that paleontologists are able to calculate how fast (or how slowly!)

TOP THREE SPEEDIEST

1st: Dromiceiomimus
Cretaceous theropod; toothless beak; long neck; stiff tail; found in Canada; up to 11.5 feet (3.5 m) long; speed of 40 miles (65 km) per hour

2nd: Gallimimus
Cretaceous theropod; large eyes; stiff tail; found in Mongolia; up to 20 feet (6 m) long; speed of 35 miles (56 km) per hour

3rd: Hypsilophodon
Cretaceous plant-eater; long legs; found in U.S. and Europe; up to 6.5 feet (2 m) long; speed of 31 miles (50 km) per hour

MOST INTELLIGENT OF ALL

Dinosaurs are often portrayed in stories and films as huge, lumbering creatures, stupidly crashing through the undergrowth. It is true that many dinosaurs had small brains. But some species, particularly the small meat-eaters, were very crafty. They had to be, in order to catch their prey and survive.

The pack of **Troodon** had no trouble hiding behind the forest's trees and in the undergrowth. At only 6.5 feet (2 m) long, they were well-concealed by thick, low-growing ferns. And even though it was nearly dark, their keen eyesight could pick out a lone victim, browsing for its evening meal. Suddenly, the **Troodon** pounced, gripping their unfortunate victim with their hand claws. The poor creature struggled in vain, for out came the **Troodon**'s sickle claws, hidden on one toe of each of their feet. The dying beast was soon cut to pieces.

Although a whole **Troodon** skeleton has never been found — only a few bones and teeth have been unearthed so far — paleontologists can still piece together enough information to show what this crafty creature would have looked like. They can also estimate the size of its brain from similarities to more complete dinosaur skeletons.

Brain tissue, of course, is soft and rots quickly, but a dinosaur's braincase has frequently survived in fossil form. Many experts believe **Troodon** had quite a large brain, and that it was one of the most intelligent dinosaurs that ever existed.

Big-brained

The large brain may also account for **Troodon**'s well-developed eyesight. Scientists think it even may have hunted like a cat does — using darkness and stealth to creep up on victims.

Some experts have also theorized that if **Troodon** had a chance to evolve more fully, its hands may have developed well enough to be able to manipulate objects — one of the skills that first separated humans from other animals.

TOP THREE BRAINIEST

1st: Troodon
Cretaceous theropod;
large eyes; found in North
America; 6.5 feet (2 m) long

2nd: Compsognathus
Jurassic theropod; found in
Europe; 2 feet (60 cm) long;
smallest dinosaur

3rd: Coelurus
Jurassic theropod; found
in North America; 6 feet
(1.8 m) long; small dinosaur

MEET THE SMALL-BRAINED

Compared to today's humans, most dinosaurs did not possess much brain-power, but they had enough to survive for millions of years. Even the least intelligent — Stegosaurus among them — were bright enough to know how to find food, breed, and try to defend themselves.

A group of **Stegosaurus** ambled into the forest clearing. They were not sure where they were going, but knew instinctively that, if they kept on plodding long enough, they would come across some tasty ferns and a river from which to have a refreshing drink. Meanwhile, they would skirt the clearing and try to stay hidden.

These harmless Jurassic plant-eaters were no match for the crafty predators that sometimes cruised in packs through the trees, looking for an easy meal. But they could often fight off a lone attacker with a sideways swipe of their spiked tails.

Just a little thick

If a dinosaur of **Stegosaurus**'s size — 30 feet (9 m) long — had been endowed with a brain in the same proportion to its body weight as a human's, it would not have been able to carry its head around! Its brain was probably just the size of a walnut. Even the most intelligent dinosaurs' brains weighed only about 2 pounds (1 kg) and amounted to only a tiny fraction of their body weight.

In a similar manner of thinking, the brain of a large sauropod, such as the giant, 50-ton **Brachiosaurus**, which also roamed Earth in Jurassic times, was very small for the size of its body. In fact, it was about the same as if you had a brain that weighed less than one of your toenails!

In addition, the "thinking" part of the brain — called the cerebrum — of dinosaurs, such as **Stegosaurus** or **Brachiosaurus**, was probably only a tiny percentage of the entire brain.

TOP THREE SMALL-BRAINED

1st: Stegosaurus
Jurassic plant-eater; found in North America; 30 feet (9 m) long; tiny head; spiked tail; plated back for temperature control; brain the size of a walnut

2nd: Diplodocus
Jurassic sauropod; found in North America; 88 feet (27 m) long; whiplash tail; long, snakelike neck ending in slim, small head; weighed about 10 tons

3rd: Brachiosaurus
Jurassic sauropod; found in North America and Tanzania, Africa; 82 feet (25 m) long; weighed 50 tons; lengthy neck, small head with tiny brain; one of the heaviest

It could be argued that if plant-eaters had had bigger brains, they might have been able to do more to avoid being eaten by predators. But, in fact, most large herbivores were ill-equipped physically to run, hide, or face a pack, or even a single attacker, on equal terms. As a result, increased brain power may not have helped them much.

However, enough dinosaurs of all degrees of intelligence survived long enough to keep their species alive for a greater amount of time than humans have inhabited Earth up to the present.

Dinosaurs reigned over the prehistoric world for some 165 million years; humans have been around for only a mere one million years.

19

BIG EATERS

Not surprisingly, large creatures need large meals to survive, but the amount of food a sizable dinosaur had to eat to survive was positively staggering!

Apatosaurus stopped chomping the lush vegetation along the treetops of the Jurassic forest and swung its long neck down to look at its front feet. If it was not careful, its pillarlike legs might disappear in a pile of droppings left by another sauropod. What a large heap it was!

The dinosaur that had produced it earlier that day had probably chomped its way through an incredible 440 pounds (200 kg) of vegetation — over twice the weight of a fairly tall and well-built adult male human being of today.

Suddenly, there was a muffled sound. The large creature moved its legs out of the way of the smelly mass and looked down. A small **Othnelia**, only 4.5 feet (1.4 m) long, was near the **Apatosaurus**'s feet and about to step into the droppings while looking for low-growing ferns. Fortunately, the frightening sight of the **Apatosaurus** steered the **Othnelia** off this sticky course.

Coprolite clues

Dinosaurs were either meat-eaters (carnivores) or plant-eaters (herbivores). Paleontologists can accurately assess what each species of dinosaur ate by examining their fossilized droppings, known as coprolites.

Some paleontologists claim that a really large carnivore, such as Cretaceous **Giganotosaurus**, may have eaten its way through huge amounts of flesh every week to satisfy its constant appetite. But it was the enormous Jurassic sauropods, such as **Brachiosaurus** and **Apatosaurus**, that are still the world-champion eaters. In fact, there may never be other creatures to inhabit Earth with such hearty appetites!

TOP THREE BIG-EATERS

1st: Brachiosaurus
Jurassic sauropod; found in North America and Tanzania, Africa; 50 tons; gargantuan appetite; high-placed nostrils; not very smart

2nd: Apatosaurus
Jurassic sauropod; found in North America; over 20 tons; huge appetite; formerly known by the name *Brontosaurus*

3rd: Damalasaurus
Jurassic sauropod; found in China; giraffelike with very long neck; possibly weighed up to 20 tons; much like **Brachiosaurus**

CLAWS!

Many types of dinosaurs had claws. Some carnivores even had a fearsome array of talons on their limbs to grab and tear prey. Several plant-eaters used either hand claws or a single toe claw as defensive weapons to ward off predators.

An unearthly shriek shattered the peace and quiet of the Late Cretaceous afternoon. A small herd of **Tenontosaurus**, grazing on plains in what is now North America, curiously craned their long necks and saw something terrifying. One of their group had strayed a little too far from the safety of the herd and was being torn to pieces by a hungry pack of **Deinonychus**.

Deadly weapons

Several of the predators — only 10 feet (3 m) long and one-tenth the size of a **Tenontosaurus** — were crawling all over the fallen giant, gouging large lumps of flesh from its body with their sickle-shaped toe claws.

Deinonychus's most fearsome weapon was the huge claw on its second toe, which it could bend upward to clear the ground as it ran.

Like all meat-eaters, it had claws on all of its fingers and toes, too.

Most theropods, such as **Deinonychus**, walked upright. So the claws on their hands could be long and curved, but they could not interfere with their movement when walking or running. However, sauropods moved around on all fours most of the time, so the claws on both the hands and feet of these dinosaurs were blunt and flat — except for one! Growing from the thumb on each of a sauropod's hands was a stocky claw with a razor-sharp edge.

As plant-eaters, however, sauropods such as **Apatosaurus** would not have needed this weapon to catch prey. Instead, the sharp claw served as a weapon that could be used, if necessary, to fight off a hungry carnivore that wanted a meal of flesh.

Thumb spikes

The bulky plant-eater **Iguanodon**, meanwhile, had a particularly impressive spiked thumb on each hand that it would use to tear out the throat of an attacker with one well-aimed slash.

Another of the most magnificent claws belonged to **Baryonyx**, a dinosaur from Cretaceous times, which was discovered along with most of its skeleton in a clay pit in southern England in 1983. This weapon measured about 12 inches (30 cm) around the outer rim of its curve, making it look like a giant fishhook. **Baryonyx** would certainly have used this feature to catch and kill its prey. Scientists also believe that, since **Baryonyx** lived mainly in wet lowland areas, it could have skewered passing fish swimming in local rivers with this claw. Dinosaurs were definitely well-armed creatures if they were lucky enough to have such impressive claws!

TOP THREE SLASHERS

1st: Deinonychus
Cretaceous theropod; found in North America; 10 feet (3 m) long with a switchblade claw on each second toe

2nd: Iguanodon
Cretaceous plant-eater; found in North America and Europe; 30 feet (9 m) long with spiked thumbs

3rd: Baryonyx
Cretaceous fish-eater; found in England; curved hand claw

POWERFUL TAILS

Dinosaur tails came in all shapes and sizes and evolved to suit particular needs. Fast runners had rigid tails, which they used to keep their balance. Some otherwise defenseless plant-eaters, meanwhile, had armored bodies and even clubbed or whiplash tails, which they could use to deal a predator a hefty blow.

The two **Ankylosaurus** stood face to face, and both raised their clubbed tails in a threatening gesture. They were males and, at the start of the mating season, were fighting over who would lead the herd and mate with most of the females. The two lumps of solid bone at the end of their tails were each about 3 feet (1 m) in diameter. These built-in clubs could deliver a mighty whack to rivals within the herd.

These tail weapons, of course, also would have been useful when predators approached. They could be swung sideways to knock even an enemy as large as **Tyrannosaurus rex** off its feet.

Fatal blows

Several plant-eaters had tail weapons with which to defend themselves. Late Jurassic **Kentrosaurus**, for example, would turn its back on an attacker and swing its tail upward. Long spikes at the tail's end would gouge the predator's soft underbelly, or possibly deliver a fatal blow. **Diplodocus**, meanwhile, would crack its 30-foot (9-m)-long tapering tail like a whip to lash out at a would-be predator. **Shunosaurus**, 30 feet (9 m) long, from what is now China, took no chances. Its tail had four spikes and a club, which it used for self-defense.

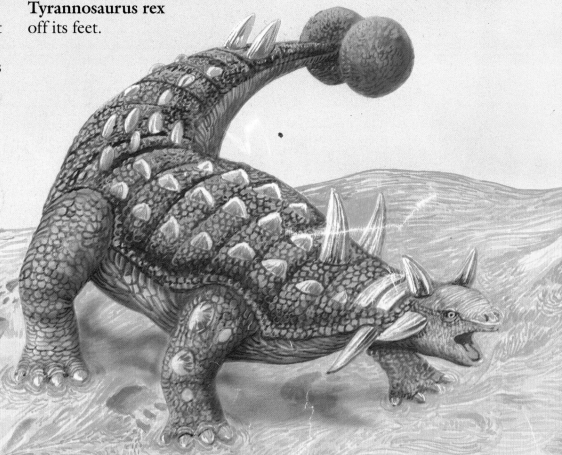

Not all strong tails served as weapons, however. Some smaller, speedier dinosaurs had rigid tails that they could hold out straight behind to keep their balance as they ran.

TOP THREE TAILS

1st: Ankylosaurus
Cretaceous plant-eater; found in North America; up to 35 feet (10.7 m) long, with a huge clubbed tail

2nd: Shunosaurus
Jurassic sauropod; found in China; 30 feet (9 m) long, with a unique spiked and clubbed tail

3rd: Diplodocus
Jurassic sauropod; found in North America; up to 88 feet (27 m) long, with a tapering, whiplash tail

TERRIFIC TEETH

No dinosaur ever had its food served up on a plate, so both meat- and plant-eaters needed strong sets of teeth to tear leathery flesh from bones or to rip tough twigs off of trees.

An **Albertosaurus** sniffed the air. It could smell the scent of a carcass — just what it was looking for! There lay the remains of a **Triceratops**, the victim of a pack of smaller predators that had been scared off by the approach of this larger creature.

Albertosaurus had not eaten that day, so it was pleased to find this food. Like **Tyrannosaurus rex**, it had rows of serrated teeth that could easily tear what was left of the fallen prey's tough flesh.

Most carnivorous dinosaurs had sharp teeth that were well-adapted for tearing meat.

Fanglike teeth were positioned at the front of their jaws, with rows of large, pointed ones behind. Some even had backward-facing teeth, such as those found in the jaw fossils of **Gorgosaurus**, which gave a victim little chance of escape, once hooked.

Straight and narrow

Some of the largest teeth of all probably belonged to **Carcharodontosaurus**, which once roamed the northern deserts of prehistoric Africa. This great carnivore had straight teeth, like a shark, set into massive jawbones. Experts say this dinosaur used its teeth to bite out neat chunks of meat, instead of tearing at the victim's flesh.

Dinosaurs that ate only plants, meanwhile, had teeth that were more suited to their diets. Some — **Iguanodon**, for example — ate mostly tough, chewy plant food, such as twigs and pine cones. They would grind up their food between rows of flat-edged teeth. Other plant-eaters, such as plated **Stegosaurus** and tanklike **Ankylosaurus**, preferred softer vegetation and had smaller, leaf-shaped teeth that worked with their more delicate diet. The hadrosaur family of dinosaurs — among them **Edmontosaurus**, which lived in what is now Canada during Cretaceous times — had no teeth at all at the front of their jaws, but they had up to a thousand tiny, diamond-shaped teeth embedded farther back. These teeth, which were only 0.5-1 inch (1-2.5 cm) long, acted as a vegetable grater for grinding their food.

Replacement teeth

With all this chewing and tearing, you might expect that dinosaur teeth eventually would either have worn down or broken off. You would be right, but dinosaurs did not starve to death as a result! They simply grew new sets of teeth as replacements for the old ones, so they could continue chomping furiously, just as they had done before!

Some carnivores may not have used their huge teeth to chew on smaller prey, instead swallowing the prey whole and risking severe indigestion in their feeding frenzy. These enormous meat-eaters had voracious appetites!

TOP THREE GNASHERS

1st: Carcharodontosaurus
Cretaceous theropod; found in northern Africa; about 26 feet (8 m) long with a big head and massive, sharklike fangs; lightly built for its size and probably fast on its feet

2nd: Tyrannosaurus rex
Cretaceous theropod; found in North America and eastern Asia; about 39 feet (12 m) long; 7-inch (18-cm)-long teeth that were serrated like steak knives; vast jaws; weighed up to 7 tons

3rd: Albertosaurus
Cretaceous theropod; found in the United States and Canada; about 26 feet (8 m) long with backward-pointing, serrated teeth; much like **Tyrannosaurus rex** but smaller in build

THE LOUDEST DINOSAURS

Most animals produce sounds of some sort to communicate, and dinosaurs were probably no exception. There is some evidence, however, that some made much more noise than others.

Never had there been such a trumpeting and bellowing in the Cretaceous forest! Silence usually reigned, broken only by the sound of plant-eaters munching through tough vegetation, or the shriek of a victim being brought down by a hungry predator. But now that a herd of **Parasaurolophus** had moved into the territory, there was no peace.

What an unusual-looking bunch they were! Each elongated skull had a huge, horn-shaped bone that stretched upward from the front of the head and stuck out 4.5 feet (1.5 m) behind. Paleontologists believe that **Parasaurolophus** must have produced the loudest noises ever heard in the prehistoric world.

Even the deep, throaty roar of giant meat-eaters, such as **Tyrannosaurus rex**, would have seemed insignificant next to **Parasaurolophus**'s call.

Warning blasts

Paleontologists believe, through close study of **Parasaurolophus**'s fossils, that a difference in the size of their crests may have marked the males from the females. Their bellowing may have been either a mating call or a warning of imminent danger.

Parasaurolophus, like all the hadrosaurs, ate plants. The slow-moving herbivore was easy prey for hungry carnivores. But a few short blasts through its crest would have been enough for one creature to alert a forest of foraging **Parasaurolophus**, which could then escape.

It was **Parasaurolophus**'s plant-eating habits that first confused paleontologists as to why it had such an extraordinary crest, full of tubes connected to its respiratory system. Some thought **Parasaurolophus** may have used the hollow crest as a kind of snorkel while it fed on underwater vegetation; others thought the tubes running up and down inside it were extra nostrils to help this huge creature breathe.

Horn concertos

Looking closer, however, scientists discovered that there was no opening at the end of the crest. This meant experts had to revise their opinions and continue their investigations. So they blew through its fossilized skull and discovered that **Parasaurolophus** must have been able to produce the loudest horn concertos imaginable!

TOP THREE LOUDEST

1st: Parasaurolophus
Cretaceous plant-eater; found in North America; boomed through head crest

2nd: Giganotosaurus
Cretaceous theropod; found in Argentina, in South America; deep roar

3rd: Compsognathus
Jurassic theropod; found in Europe; only 2 feet (60 cm) long; though very small, its cry may have been extremely high

GLOSSARY

array — an orderly grouping or arrangement of materials.

browse — to feed on the tender shoots, twigs, and leaves of trees and shrubs.

bulky — having great size or weight; thick and heavy.

camouflaged — colored, marked, or shaped in a way that blends in with the background.

cannibal — a creature that eats its own kind. Many paleontologists believe that **Coelophysis** was cannibalistic.

carcass — the body of a dead animal; corpse.

carnivore — a meat-eater.

cerebrum — the large upper part of the brain that is considered the center of thinking.

coprolites — fossilized dinosaur dung, or droppings. Scientists can tell what the dinosaurs ate by examining coprolites.

Cretaceous times — the final era of the dinosaurs, lasting from 144-65 million years ago.

evolved — adapted and changed over a period of time to suit changing environments.

forelimbs — the front arms, legs, fins, or wings of an animal.

fossilized — embedded and preserved in rocks, resin, or other material.

gargantuan — very large; huge.

gastrolith — one of the numerous small stones swallowed by certain types of plant-eating dinosaurs, such as **Seismosaurus**, to help with the digestion of tough plant material.

hadrosaur — a member of a group of duck-billed dinosaurs.

herbivore — a plant-eater.

instinctively — behaving in a way that is natural, or automatic, rather than learned.

Jurassic times — the middle era of the dinosaurs, lasting from 213-144 million years ago.

manipulate — to operate or hold something with your hands.

paleontologist — a scientist who studies geologic periods of the past as they are known from fossil remains.

predator — an animal that hunts other animals for food.

primitive — living in or having to do with earliest times; not highly developed or evolved.

pterosaur — a member of a group of extinct flying reptiles.

sauropods — long-necked, plant-eating dinosaurs, such as **Apatosaurus**, mainly from Jurassic times.

serrated — edged with notches or teeth, like the blade of a knife.

sickle — a tool with a curved blade used for cutting. Some dinosaurs had deadly, sickle-shaped claws to kill prey or to defend themselves.

sinewy — tough; strong and well-muscled.

skewer — to stab with or fasten something onto a sharp tool or claw.

stocky — having a short and heavy build.

tapering — becoming more narrow; coming to a point.

theropod — a type of meat-eating, bipedal dinosaur.

thicket — a thick growth of shrubs, bushes, or small trees.

Triassic times — the first era of the dinosaurs, lasting from 249-213 million years ago.

undergrowth — the bushes and smaller plants that grow under large trees in a forest.

voracious — having a huge, ravenous appetite.

MORE BOOKS TO READ

Amazing Dinosaur Facts. Robert A. Bell (Western)

The Best Book of Dinosaurs. Christopher Maynard (Kingfisher)

Dinosaurs. David Norman (Knopf)

Dinosaurs of All Sizes. Alvin Granowsky (Steck-Vaughn)

Dinosaurs and How They Lived. Steve Parker (Dorling Kindersley)

Dinosaurs: Monster Reptiles of a Bygone Era. Eulalia García (Gareth Stevens)

Giant Dinosaurs. Peter Dodson (Scholastic)

The New Dinosaur Collection (series). (Gareth Stevens)

Supergiants: The Biggest Dinosaurs. Don Lessem (Little, Brown & Company)

Weird and Wonderful Dinosaur Facts. Monica Russo (Sterling)

When Dinosaurs Ruled the Earth. Dougal Dixon (Gareth Stevens)

World of Dinosaurs (series). (Gareth Stevens)

VIDEOS

Did Comets Kill The Dinosaurs? (Gareth Stevens)

Digging Up Dinosaurs. (Great Plains National Instructional Television Library)

Dinosaur! (series). (Arts & Entertainment Network)

Dinosaurs: The Age of Reptiles. (Phoenix/BFA Films & Video)

Dinosaurs: Remains to Be Seen. (Public Media, Inc.)

Dinosaurs: The Terrible Lizards. (AIMS Media)

The Last Word on Dinosaurs. (Films for the Humanities and Sciences)

Nova: The Case of the Flying Dinosaur. (Live Home Video)

WEB SITES

pubs.usgs.gov/gip/dinosaurs

www.ZoomDinosaurs.com

www.dinodon.com/

www.dinosociety.org

www.ucmp.berkeley.edu/

www.dinofest.org/

Due to the dynamic nature of the internet, some web sites stay current longer than others. To find additional web sites, use a reliable search engine with one or more of the following keywords to help you locate more information about dinosaurs. Keywords: *Cretaceous, dinosaurs, fossils, Jurassic, paleontology, prehistoric, Triassic.*

INDEX